Robert Quackenbush

James Madison & Dolley Madison

AND THEIR TIMES

Pippin Press

Published by Pippin Press, 229 East 85th Street,
Gracie Station Box #92,
New York, N.Y. 10028

Printed in the United States by Horowitz/Rae
Book Manufacturers, Inc.
10 9 8 7 6 5 4 3 2 1

Library of Congress Cataloging-in-Publication Data

Quackenbush, Robert M.
    James Madison and Dolley Madison and their times / written and
illustrated by Robert Quackenbush.
        p.   cm.
    Summary: Describes the background of the country's fourth
president and his wife and their role in the young nation's history.
    ISBN 0-945912-18-8
    1. Madison, James, 1751–1836—Juvenile literature.   2. Madison,
Dolley, 1768–1849—Juvenile literature.   3. Presidents—United
States—Biography—Juvenile literature.   4. Presidents—United
States—Wives—Biography—Juvenile literature.   [1. Madison,
James, 1751–1836.   2. Madison, Dolley, 1768–1849.
3. Presidents.   4. First ladies.]   I. Title.
E342.Q33   1992
973.5′1′0922—dc20
[B]   92-24505
                                                            CIP
                                                             AC

For Piet
&
Margie

and for
the students, teachers, and parents
in Greensboro, North Carolina
with deepest thanks and appreciation
for their
inspiration and hospitality.
R.Q.

JAMES MADISON GREW UP LOVING BOOKS.

James Madison was the firstborn of James Madison, Sr.'s and Nelly Conway Madison's twelve children. Seven of the Madison children did not live past infancy. James himself was sickly from the time of his birth on March 16, 1751, at Port Conway, Orange County, Virginia. Virginia in those days was one of thirteen colonies in America that were ruled by the British. James was raised on his father's 4,000-acre plantation, called Montpelier. Being the oldest son, he inherited the mansion and the land when his father died in 1801.

With other Virginia boys, James liked to ride and shoot, but he did not participate in most other outdoor sports because of his small size and poor health. Instead, he enjoyed reading books. He received his early education at home from tutors. Then, when he was eleven, his parents sent him to a celebrated school seventy miles from home. The school was run by Donald Robertson, who had been educated in Scotland. Under Robertson's guidance, James learned Latin and Greek, French, algebra and geometry, geography, and the classic literature. Years later Madison wrote, "All that I have been in life I owe largely to that man."

Madison attended Robertson's school until he was sixteen. Then he returned home and was tutored for two years by Rev. Thomas Martin, who was in charge of a nearby church. After that, he decided to go to the College of New Jersey (renamed Princeton University in 1896), where Martin had studied. The president of the college, Dr. John Witherspoon, encouraged the students to read widely, to write about complicated ideas, to join in debates, and to deliver speeches. Madison studied hard and completed the standard four year course of study in two years. Princeton had molded him for public life.

In 1775, Madison represented Orange County as a delegate at a Virginia convention in Williamsburg. The convention was formed to decide on a new government for Virginia which would be independent of England. For years the colonists wanted to be free of British tyranny. They resented paying many unjust taxes without being represented in Parliament. War had already broken out in Massachusetts. At the assembly, Madison learned about politics from Virginia's distinguished political leaders. From Thomas Jefferson and George Mason he learned about writing documents. From Patrick Henry, whose passionate plea, "Give me liberty or give me death," has echoed down through the ages, he learned about great public speaking.

YOUNG JAMES MADISON STUDIES WITH DR. JOHN WITHERSPOON AT PRINCETON

MADISON SPEAKS BEFORE THE 1775 VIRGINIA ASSEMBLY WHERE HE BECOMES FRIENDS WITH THOMAS JEFFERSON.

During the convention Madison and Jefferson established a close friendship that was to last for fifty years. In appearance they were opposites. Madison was short (five feet, four inches), shy, and dressed only in black. Jefferson was tall (six feet, two inches), lively, and dressed in mismatched clothing. But they shared a common background, for they grew up in neighboring counties and had received similar educations. Above all, both were devoted to the cause of liberty.

In the spring of 1776, Jefferson left for Philadelphia to write the Declaration of Independence for the Second Continental Congress (the colonies' governing body). This historical document declared the colonies a free and independent nation. When it was signed by Congress on July 4, 1776, the Revolutionary War officially began. George Washington, commander-in-chief of the Continental Army, pleaded with the colonies to send their best men to Congress to plan ways to send supplies to his starving, ragged army. Virginia sent James Madison. Madison convinced Congress to pass a federal tax bill to raise money for food, clothing, and other supplies for the troops. This was not easy to do since British taxation without representation in Parliament was what caused the war in the first place.

America won the war in June 1783 and the colonies became thirteen states that were loosely joined together under a central (or federal) government, called a confederacy. The confederacy was formed by the laws of the Articles of Confederation that were created by the Second Continental Congress in 1776, but the states remained independent of one another.

After the war, Madison returned to his post in the Virginia legislature. Three years later, in 1786, the states began having differences with the federal government over taxes. At the same time debt-ridden farmers led an uprising in Massachusetts (called Shays' Rebellion) because they were about to lose their farms and they felt they were not represented well enough in the state legislature. Massachusetts' own army, known as a militia, had to put down the rebels without the help of the Continental Congress, which was too weak to respond to such emergencies. Other states became frightened that Congress would not be able to protect them when rebellions occurred in their own states. It became obvious to everyone that a new constitution was needed to replace the Articles of Confederation in order to unify the states under a more powerful central government. A date was set for a Constitutional Convention to meet on May 25, 1787.

NOW THAT THE FEDERAL TAX BILL HAS BEEN PASSED, I THINK IT WOULD BE A MISTAKE FOR THE STATES TO DELAY PAYING TAXES FOR A YEAR.

LOOK! YOU GOT YOUR WAY WITH THE BILL! SO WAIT A YEAR!

PATRICK HENRY DOESN'T FOOL AROUND WITH WORDS.

HE'S WHA YOU CALL FORCEF SPEAK!

AN UPRISING IN MASSACHUSETTS IN 1786 CAUSES GREAT CONCERN AMONG THE STATES.

JAMES MADISON RECORDS EVERYTHING THAT IS DISCUSSED AT THE CONSTITUTIONAL CONVENTION.

To prepare for the convention, Madison read many books about governments that were similar to the American confederacy. Thomas Jefferson, who was in Paris at the time, sent him books on ancient Greek and Roman governments. From all the reading, Madison found out that confederacies failed when the central government was too weak and the states were overly strong. He set to work drafting a plan for a new constitution to present to the Constitutional Convention which would prevent this from happening to the fledgling nation.

George Washington led the convention of delegates from the states. Only Rhode Island did not attend because its leaders feared that the larger states would have more power. Madison's proposal—called the Virginia plan—became the focus of the convention. His plan was a system of checks and balances consisting of three branches to keep the central government from becoming too weak and the states from becoming too powerful. The first was the legislative branch (the Congress) to make laws. The second was the executive branch (the presidency) to carry out the laws. The third was the judicial branch (the Supreme Court) to interpret the laws. After many debates and arguments for and against Madison's plan, plus 161 speeches by Madison himself to defend it, the new constitution was signed by 55 delegates on September 15, 1787.

..THE CONSTANT AIM IS TO DIVIDE AND ARRANGE THE SEVERAL OFFICES IN SUCH A MANNER AS THAT EACH MAY BE A CHECK ON THE OTHER...

HOW DID MADISON KNOW SO MUCH?

HE LOVED READING.

COMIC BOOKS, TOO?

MADISON, JAY, AND HAMILTON WRITE ESSAYS EXPLAINING THE CONSTITUTION TO THE PUBLIC

After the delegates signed the Constitution, each state legislature had to approve it before it could become law. The states wanted a guarantee that a Bill of Rights would be added to the Constitution before they would approve it. Madison drafted twelve rights, including freedom of speech, the press, and religion. Then he, Alexander Hamilton, and John Jay wrote 85 newspaper articles to explain and gain support for the Constitution. The essays, now called *The Federalist* papers (federalism means the unification of the states under a central government), had a positive influence on the voters. By July 1788, ten states—all but New York, North Carolina, and Rhode Island—had given their approval to the Constitution. The new government was called the United States of America and Madison came to be known as the "father of the Constitution."

The next step was for people to vote for a president and members of the two houses of Congress (the Senate and House of Representatives). George Washington was elected president. The Senate wanted to call him "His Highness, the President of the United States of America, and Protector of the Rights of the Same." Fortunately, James Madison, who had been elected to the House, suggested a title that won the approval of both the House and Senate, which was simply "the president of the United States."

Washington, the first president of the United States of America, served two terms. He declined a third term and John Adams was elected to succeed him. At the time, Congress was divided into two camps—the Federalist camp and the Republican camp. This was the beginning of the two-party system still in existence today. Adams, Hamilton, and their supporters were for the aristocrats and referred to themselves as the Federalists (now called the Republican party). Jefferson, Madison, and their supporters were for the common man and referred to themselves as Republicans (now called the Democratic party).

Madison knew that since he belonged to the Republican camp, he would not be wanted in the new government that had the Federalist Adams as president. Therefore, after twenty years in public office, he decided it was time to retire. But he did not want to return to Montpelier alone. He was forty-three years old and he wanted to be married. Through Aaron Burr, a classmate at Princeton, Madison was introduced to a pretty, twenty-six-year-old widow named Dolley Payne Todd. Burr had known her since she was a young girl when he lived at her mother's boarding house. Madison went to pay her a call.

JAMES MADISON VISITS DOLLEY PAYNE TODD.

DOLLEY PRACTICES BEING A HOSTESS WITH HER YOUNGER SIBLINGS AT SCOTCHTOWN.

Dolley Payne was born on May 20, 1768, when her parents John and Mary Payne were visiting friends in Greensboro, North Carolina. She was raised on a plantation in Virginia, called Scotchtown, with two older brothers, three younger sisters, and two younger brothers. Her family were Quakers who wore plain, dark clothes and did not engage in dancing, card-games, or other "vanities" that were against their religion. But they enjoyed good food and plenty of it, although it was served with simple utensils on the plainest of china.

After the Revolutionary War, Dolley's father, like many other Quakers, became concerned about slavery. He freed his slaves and sold Scotchtown. He took his family to Philadelphia to start a starch manufacturing company. But his business failed. Mary Payne opened a boarding house to support the family when debts went unpaid. Government officials roomed and took meals there. Dolley and her sisters learned about being good hostesses from their mother. Mary Payne taught them that a combination of lively conversation and good food was the secret of successful entertaining.

Dolley blossomed into a beautiful young woman with blue eyes, black curly hair, and a creamy complexion. In 1790, at the age of twenty-one, she married a young Quaker lawyer named John Todd. The wedding was a simple affair with no music or dancing. Two years afterward, in 1792, Dolley and Todd's first child, a son they named Payne, was born.

The following year, in August 1793, Dolley gave birth to a second son, William Temple. That same summer Philadelphia was stricken by a yellow fever epidemic (for which a cure was found a century later) that killed 5,000 people. Philadelphians did not know that the yellow fever germs were being carried by mosquitoes that were breeding in nearby swamps. Todd sent Dolley and the children to the country while he stayed behind to help his aged parents who could not leave the city. Then Todd was stricken with yellow fever. He rushed to the country for a last look at his beloved Dolley and the children. Just as he got to the house, he collapsed and died. The tragedy was not over. Baby William suddenly died from an unknown cause the same day. Dolley herself became ill (not from yellow fever) but she survived and so did Payne. She moved back to the city. One year later the young widow met James Madison.

LL AND DYING, JOHN TODD FLEES PHILADELPHIA TO SEE HIS FAMILY ONE LAST TIME.

THE WEDDING OF JAMES MADISON AND DOLLEY PAYNE TODD

Six months after they met, James Madison and Dolley Payne Todd were married on September 15, 1794. They were very happy together. Dolley was especially happy to have a kind, loving man to be a father to her son, Payne. She gave up her Quaker life and began wearing elegant dresses and turbans. They settled at Montpelier to farm and entertain friends.

In the next presidential election, in 1800, the people were so unhappy with Adams and the Federalists that they voted for Thomas Jefferson and the Republicans. As soon as Jefferson took office as third president of the United States, he wanted Madison to be his secretary of state to negotiate with diplomats that came to America. Also, since Jefferson was a widower, he asked Dolley to serve as his official hostess at the presidential mansion in the new capital city, Washington, D.C. The Madisons accepted the honors. Dolley gave dinner parties and balls at the mansion for important statesmen of the time and soon became Washington's outstanding social leader. Madison's greatest achievement was helping Jefferson to convince France, in 1803, to sell the Louisiana Territory to the United States for only $15,000,000. With this purchase, the United States doubled in size.

27

PERRY'S VICTORY ON LAKE ERIE

Jefferson served two presidential terms. Then, on March 4, 1809, James Madison became the fourth president of the United States, after defeating Federalist Charles Pinckney in the November 1808 election. Three years later, America faced another war with England. It started when England and France began capturing neutral American ships and taking their cargoes and crews. The French and English were at war with each other at the time. Neither country wanted American ships to trade with the other. At last, in July 1811, France released all captured American ships. But England, which held 6,200 seamen, still refused to stop taking crews from American ships to work on their own ships. Madison was forced to sign an official declaration of war with England on July 17, 1812.

The War of 1812 began badly. The Americans had poorly trained troops, bungling generals, and no warships on the Great Lakes to protect the United States from attack by British forces in Canada. In the summer of 1813, after terrible losses to the American army, Madison replaced incompetent generals with effective leaders and sent ships to the Great Lakes. Soon after, America's Admiral Oliver Hazard Perry won an amazing naval victory on Lake Erie. Shortly after Perry's victory, American troops held the British at bay in the north.

By 1814, England had won the war with France and was able to use more military might against the United States. On August 23, fifty British ships with 4,000 troops dropped anchor two day's march from Washington. The soldiers began a slow advance toward the capital. At midnight the same day, a messenger woke up the Madisons to warn them that the British were coming. Madison rode on horseback to check the city's defenses at the outskirts of town. He found inexperienced local troops running around helter-skelter.

Meanwhile, at the presidential mansion, Dolley hurried to save what she could before the British got there. She ripped down some velvet draperies in the oval room. She had a servant pack them on a wagon with a clock, some silver, and Gilbert Stuart's full-length portrait of George Washington. With sounds of gunfire getting closer and closer, she quickly set out a dinner for Madison. Then she fled to take a ferry across the Potomac River. Soon afterward Madison returned to the mansion to make certain his wife was safely gone. Seeing that she was, and with no time to eat the dinner she had left for him, he galloped to meet her in Virginia. After he left, British Commander Cockburn stormed into the mansion and ate the meal Dolley had set out for Madison. Then he ordered his men to set fire to the mansion and Washington.

I HOPE THAT THE BRITISH COMMANDER GOT SICK FROM THE MEAL I PREPARED. IT WOULD SERVE HIM RIGHT FOR SETTING FIRE TO THE PRESIDENTIAL MANSION.

I AGREE

I AGREE

I AGREE.

I AGREE.

I AGREE.

MEOW

DOLLEY HURRIEDLY SAVES WHAT SHE CAN FROM THE PRESIDENTIAL MANSION

O Say can you see ~~through~~ by the dawn's early light,
What so proudly, we hail'd at the twilight's last gleaming
Whose broad stripes and bright stars through the perilous fight,
O'er the ramparts we watch'd, were so gallantly streaming?
And the rocket's red glare — the bomb bursting in air
Gave proof throu...

FRANCES SCOTT KEY WRITES "THE STAR-SPANGLED BANNER."

Three days later, the British retreated. Madison rode back to find the presidential mansion a burned-out, empty shell. Most of the public buildings except the Post and Patent Offices were burnt to the ground. Some of the private houses had survived the fire. Madison and Dolley moved into one of the houses. They never lived in the presidential mansion again. Congress took up quarters in the Post and Patent Offices. Within a month of the British attack, the government was back in operation in Washington. In the meantime, the British were turned back in upper New York and at Baltimore. All through the night of September 14, British cannons fired on Baltimore's Fort McHenry. At dawn, a young man named Francis Scott Key was so moved to see the American flag still flying over the fort that he wrote the words to "The Star-Spangled Banner," our national anthem.

Still, the British continued to fight. They moved their attack to the South. They were met in New Orleans on January 8, 1815 by Andrew Jackson and 6,000 men. The British gave up the battle after losing 700 men. The Americans lost seven. Then on February 14, Madison learned more good news. England had agreed to a peace treaty. Congress voted within a day to accept the treaty. On February 17, 1815, Madison declared the war was over.

I GAVE MANY PARTIES AFTER THE WAR WAS OVER. BUT I STUCK TO MY GUNS AND PASSED AROUND A BOWL OF FRUIT AT DESERT TIME. I'M ALL FOR A HEALTHIER NATION.

I AGREE.

FRUIT?

START A RUMOR: DOLLEY MADISON INVENTED THE BANANA SPLIT.

JAMES MADISON & DOLLEY MADISON SPEND THEIR FINAL YEARS TOGETHER AT MONTPELIE

One year after the war, the Republicans won again in the election of 1816. James Monroe, another good friend of Madison, became the fifth president of the United States. After Monroe's inauguration in 1817, the Madisons stayed in Washington for a month of farewell celebrations. Madison received tributes for his many contributions to his country—the Constitution, the Bill of Rights, and the wisdom of his years as President. Even John Adams said that Madison had "acquired more glory, and established more Union, than all three predecessors, Washington, Adams, and Jefferson."

Afterward, the Madisons left for Montpelier. Although Madison never returned to Washington, he was drawn back into public issues. He corresponded with President Monroe who wrote asking for his opinion on government matters. He served as delegate from his county at an 1829 Virginia convention to write a new state constitution. He supplied Congress with historical information that ended an 1833 dispute between the North and South. But his friends from the early days were gone. Jefferson, his closest friend of fifty years, died on July 4, 1826, after saying to Madison a few weeks earlier, "To myself you have been a pillar of support through life." A decade later, Madison, ill with arthritis, died calmly at breakfast on June 28, 1836, at age 85.

Because of James Madison's enormous contributions to his country—the Constitution and the Bill of Rights—the United States endures as a great democracy, regarded all over the world today as the finest example of a country structuring a social and political order and the first universal nation (people from many lands and cultures).

Dolley Madison lived for thirteen years after her husband. During those years her son, Payne, whom Dolley had spoiled as a child, pestered her for money to pay off gambling debts. Finally, he mismanaged her estate so badly that she had to sell Montpelier and move back to Washington. When she returned to the capital she was treated like a returning queen. Congress voted for her to receive $25,000 (a large sum in those days) so she could live comfortably the rest of her days. She died peacefully, at age 81.

Madison had named Dolley to be in charge of his writings and papers, a task she took very seriously to the end of her days. A paper exists in her handwriting apparently taken down at his dictation to be read after his death. It is headed *Advice to My Country* and ends with these words:

> *The advice nearest my heart and deepest in my convictions*
> *is that the Union of the States be cherished and perpetuated.*

Notes:

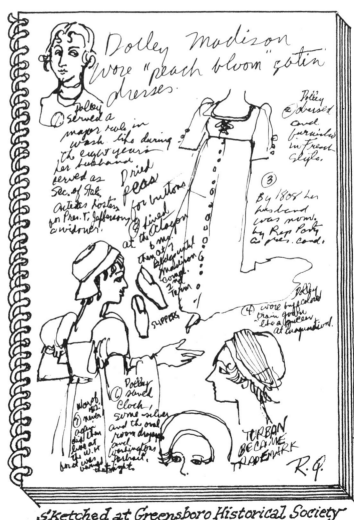

Sketched at Greensboro Historical Society
Greensboro, N.C., 1991